Usborne
Lift-the-flap

# Nativity

ISBN 0-439-68683-0

12 11 10 9 8 7 6 5 4 3 2 1        4 5 6 7 8 9/0

Printed in Singapore              46

First Scholastic printing, November 2004

Usborne
Lift-the-flap
# Nativity

Retold by Felicity Brooks

Designer and modelmaker: Jo Litchfield

Managing designer: Mary Cartwright
Photography by Howard Allman

SCHOLASTIC INC.
New York   Toronto   London   Auckland   Sydney
Mexico City   New Delhi   Hong Kong   Buenos Aires

A long time ago in the village of Nazareth there lived a carpenter. His name was Joseph.

Joseph had a wife named Mary.
Mary was expecting a baby.

Mary and Joseph had to go to Bethlehem to put their names on a register. It was a long journey.

In Bethlehem they looked for a place to stay.
Everywhere was full, apart from a stable.

That night Mary's baby
was born. She named him Jesus.
She made a bed for him in a manger.

In the hills above Bethlehem there were some shepherds. They were taking care of their flock.

Suddenly there was an amazing bright light
in the sky. The shepherds were very frightened.

It was a
beautiful,
shining angel.

"Don't be scared,"
said the angel. "I have
some good news for you.

"Tonight a baby has been
born who is the Son of God.
Go to Bethlehem and find him."

Then the light grew even brighter and the sky
was filled with beautiful, shining, singing angels.

The shepherds ran into Bethlehem
and found the baby asleep in the stable.

They kneeled down and prayed. Then they
told Mary and Joseph what the angel had said.

A long way from Bethlehem there were three Wise Men. One night they saw a very bright star.

It was moving across the sky.
The Wise Men knew it meant
something special had happened.

The Wise Men followed
the star. They rode for
many days and nights.

When they reached Bethlehem the star stopped moving. They knew this was the right place.

The Wise Men found Jesus asleep
in the hay. They laid gifts around him.

They gave him gold,
frankincense and myrrh.

The Wise Men said goodbye and went quietly away. The shepherds went around Bethlehem telling everyone the good news.

Mary held Jesus safely in her arms and thought about everything that had happened.

And that is the story
of the first Christmas
a very long time ago.